MAD LIBS®

Mad Libs In Love

By Roger Price and Leonard Stern

PSS!
PRICE STERN SLOAN

MAD LIBS
INSTRUCTIONS

MAD LIBS® is a game for people who don't like games!
It can be played by one, two, three, four, or forty.

• RIDICULOUSLY SIMPLE DIRECTIONS

In this tablet you will find stories containing blank spaces where words are
left out. One player, the READER, selects one of these stories. The READER
does not tell anyone what the story is about. Instead, he/she asks the other
players, the WRITERS, to give him/her words. These words are used to fill in
the blank spaces in the story.

• TO PLAY

The READER asks each WRITER in turn to call out a word—an adjective or
a noun or whatever the space calls for—and uses them to fill in the blank
spaces in the story. The result is a MAD LIBS® game.

When the READER then reads the completed MAD LIBS® game to the other
players, they will discover that they have written a story that is fantastic,
screamingly funny, shocking, silly, crazy, or just plain dumb—depending
upon which words each WRITER called out.

• EXAMPLE (*Before* and *After*)

"_____!" he said _____
　　　　　EXCLAMATION　　　　　　　　　　　　　　　ADVERB

as he jumped into his convertible _____ and
　　　　　　　　　　　　　　　　　　　　　　　NOUN

drove off with his _____ wife.
　　　　　　　　　　　ADJECTIVE

"_____*Ouch!*_____!" he said _____*Stupidly*_____
　　　　　EXCLAMATION　　　　　　　　　　　　　　　ADVERB

as he jumped into his convertible _____*cat*_____ and
　　　　　　　　　　　　　　　　　　　　　　　NOUN

drove off with his _____*brave*_____ wife.
　　　　　　　　　　　ADJECTIVE

In case you have forgotten what adjectives, adverbs, nouns, and verbs are, here is a quick review:

An ADJECTIVE describes something or somebody. *Lumpy, soft, ugly, messy,* and *short* are adjectives.

An ADVERB tells how something is done. It modifies a verb and usually ends in "ly." *Modestly, stupidly, greedily,* and *carefully* are adverbs.

A NOUN is the name of a person, place or thing. *Sidewalk, umbrella, bridle, bathtub,* and *nose* are nouns.

A VERB is an action word. *Run, pitch, jump,* and *swim* are verbs. Put the verbs in past tense if the directions say PAST TENSE. *Ran, pitched, jumped,* and *swam* are verbs in the past tense.

When we ask for a PLACE, we mean any sort of place: a country or city *(Spain, Cleveland)* or a room *(bathroom, kitchen.)*

An EXCLAMATION or SILLY WORD is any sort of funny sound, gasp, grunt, or outcry, like *Wow!, Ouch!, Whomp!, Ick!,* and *Gadzooks!*

When we ask for specific words, like a NUMBER, a COLOR, an ANIMAL, or a PART OF THE BODY, we mean a word that is one of those things, like *seven, blue, horse,* or *head.*

When we ask for a PLURAL, it means more than one. For example, *cat* pluralized is *cats.*

MAD LIBS® is fun to play with friends, but you can also play it by yourself! To begin with, DO NOT look at the story on the page below. Fill in the blanks on this page with the words called for. Then, using the words you've selected, fill in the blank spaces in the story.

Now you've created your own hilarious MAD LIBS® game!

HOW TO WRITE A LOVE LETTER

NOUN _____

NOUN _____

NOUN _____

NOUN _____

ADVERB _____

PLURAL NOUN _____

NOUN _____

NOUN _____

NOUN _____

ADJECTIVE _____

VERB _____

ADVERB _____

NOUN _____

ADJECTIVE _____

NOUN _____

ADVERB _____

NOUN _____

MAD LIBS
HOW TO WRITE
A LOVE LETTER

If you want to send an easy-to-read letter, fax or

e- __Milk shake__ to a loved - __sneeze__ , a dear __dog__ , or
    NOUN   NOUN   NOUN

even a business __pudding__ , you must know how to
                            NOUN

punctuate it __suprizingly__ ! Follow these easily understood
                  ADVERB

__lights__ for the proper placement of a period, a
      PLURAL NOUN

comma, a question __film__ , or an exclamation __nurse__ ,
                    NOUN   NOUN

and you'll have it made.

1) A period only comes at the end of a/an __program__ .
                                          NOUN

2) A comma is a/an __bigger__ pause in a sentence.
                     ADJECTIVE

It separates words that would be confused if they

__scream__ together.
    VERB

3) The question mark is __mindfully__ used after a
                            ADVERB

__cherry__ is asked.
  NOUN

4) The exclamation mark tells the reader that what has just

been written is urgent, significant, and __wet__ . It only
                                    ADJECTIVE

comes at the end of a __pillow__ . Now, you are __simply__
                      NOUN   ADVERB

equipped to write an easily understood love __snickers__ .
                                                            NOUN

From Mad Libs® In Love • Copyright © 2001 by Price Stern Sloan,
a division of Penguin Putnam Books for Young Readers, New York.

MAD LIBS® is fun to play with friends, but you can also play it by yourself! To begin with, DO NOT look at the story on the page below. Fill in the blanks on this page with the words called for. Then, using the words you've selected, fill in the blank spaces in the story.

Now you've created your own hilarious MAD LIBS® game!

CUPID CHAT ROOM

PLURAL NOUN ___lubricants___

NOUN ___vibrator___

NOUN ___penis___

VERB ENDING IN "ING" ___fucking___

NOUN ~~~~~ ___tongue___

NOUN ___pornstar___

PLURAL NOUN ___tits___

NOUN ___Butt hole___

NOUN ___lips___

NOUN ___a kiss___

PART OF THE BODY ___perenium / grundle___

VERB ___pull~~~~~___

NOUN ___whip___

SPANISH WORD ___amor___

PLURAL NOUN ___eyes___

PLURAL NOUN ___handcuffs___

PERSON IN ROOM ___Amy___

PLURAL NOUN ___fingers___

CUPID CHAT ROOM

Of all the Greek and Roman _____, Cupid, the
PLURAL NOUN

god of _____, is certainly the best known. Almost anyone
NOUN

you meet, from a stranger on a/an _____, to a teenager
NOUN

in the _____ mall, or even an alien from outer
VERB ENDING IN "ING"

_____, knows about Cupid. They know him to be a
NOUN

scantily clad _____ with a pair of _____ on
NOUN   PLURAL NOUN

his back and a bow and _____ in his _____. They
NOUN   NOUN

also know that if Cupid shoots a/an _____ into your
NOUN

_____, you automatically _____ in love with a
PART OF THE BODY   VERB

member of the opposite _____. Even those scholars who
NOUN

don't think of Cupid as numero _____ will admit
SPANISH WORD

that he ranks up there with Zeus, god of _____,
PLURAL NOUN

Apollo, god of _____, and _____,
PLURAL NOUN   PERSON IN ROOM

god of _____.
PLURAL NOUN

MAD LIBS® is fun to play with friends, but you can also play it by yourself! To begin with, DO NOT look at the story on the page below. Fill in the blanks on this page with the words called for. Then, using the words you've selected, fill in the blank spaces in the story.

Now you've created your own hilarious MAD LIBS® game!

MEET YOUR DREAM PERSON

PLURAL NOUN _____

ADJECTIVE _____

PLURAL NOUN _____

ADJECTIVE _____

PART OF THE BODY _____

ADVERB _____

ADJECTIVE _____

ADJECTIVE _____

NOUN _____

ADJECTIVE _____

WEIRD SOUND _____

VERB _____

NOUN _____

NOUN _____

PLURAL NOUN _____

NOUN _____.

MAD LIBS®

MEET YOUR DREAM PERSON

If you are desirous of making new _____ or
                                        PLURAL NOUN

meeting some _____ people, take a few _____
                ADJECTIVE   PLURAL NOUN

out of your _____ day and answer the following
                ADJECTIVE

questionnaire. In less time than it takes to blink a/an

_____, your life will be changed _____ by
PART OF THE BODY   ADVERB

your _____ answers.
        ADJECTIVE

• Do you ever confide in a/an _____ friend that you
                                    ADJECTIVE

  are a lonely _____?
                    NOUN

• Are you too shy and _____ to approach a stranger
                            ADJECTIVE

  and say _____?
              WEIRD SOUND

• Would you rather stay at home and _____
                                            VERB

  television than go out on a blind _____?
                                          NOUN

If you answered yes to any of these questions, you have taken

one giant _____ toward meeting the person of your
                NOUN

_____ . To make this a reality, mail the enclosed
PLURAL NOUN

self-addressed, postage-paid _____ to us immediately.
                                    NOUN

MAD LIBS® is fun to play with friends, but you can also play it by yourself! To begin with, DO NOT look at the story on the page below. Fill in the blanks on this page with the words called for. Then, using the words you've selected, fill in the blank spaces in the story.

Now you've created your own hilarious MAD LIBS® game!

SAY IT WITH FLOWERS

NOUN _____

VERB _____

NOUN _____

ADJECTIVE _____

VERB _____

PLURAL NOUN _____

ADJECTIVE _____

PLURAL NOUN _____

VERB _____

PART OF THE BODY _____

PLURAL NOUN _____

VERB ENDING WITH "S" _____

PLURAL NOUN _____

ADVERB _____

PLURAL NOUN _____

SMALL NUMBER _____

NOUN _____

MAD LIBS®

SAY IT WITH FLOWERS

A dramatic scene in a flower shop: A young man enters.

The florist approaches him.

Florist: Good morning. You are my first _____ of the
NOUN

day. How can I _____ you, sir?
VERB

Young Man: I'm taking my _____ to the _____
NOUN   ADJECTIVE

prom tonight. What do you suggest I _____ her?
VERB

Florist: A bouquet of spring _____ would be
PLURAL NOUN

very _____ .
ADJECTIVE

Young Man: I'm sorry, she's allergic to daisies and _____ .
PLURAL NOUN

They make her _____ her _____ off.
VERB   PART OF THE BODY

Florist: How about long-stemmed _____ ?
PLURAL NOUN

Young Man: Can't do that, either. Her father _____
VERB ENDING WITH "S"

roses. He has more rose bushes than you can count on both

your _____ .
PLURAL NOUN

Florist: Then how about a corsage? Corsages are _____
ADVERB

perfect! Young _____ love them.
PLURAL NOUN

Young Man: Cool! What can I get for _____ cents?
SMALL NUMBER

Florist: Dirt. But I'll put it in a gift _____ for you.
NOUN

MAD LIBS® is fun to play with friends, but you can also play it by yourself!
To begin with, DO NOT look at the story on the page below. Fill in the blanks
on this page with the words called for. Then, using the words you've selected,
fill in the blank spaces in the story.

Now you've created your own hilarious MAD LIBS® game!

ON DATING A TWIN

NOUN _____

ADVERB _____

PLURAL NOUN _____

PLURAL NOUN _____

PLURAL NOUN _____

PLURAL NOUN _____

PLURAL NOUN _____

NOUN _____

NOUN _____

VERB ENDING IN "ING" _____

PLURAL NOUN _____

PLURAL NOUN _____

PERSON IN ROOM (MALE) _____

PERSON IN ROOM (FEMALE)_____

MAD LIBS®
ON DATING A TWIN

Going out with an identical _____ is _____ freaky!
NOUN   ADVERB

No one can tell twins apart, not even their _____
PLURAL NOUN

or close _____. Everything about them is the
PLURAL NOUN

same. The color of their _____, the shape of their
PLURAL NOUN

_____, the shape of their chiseled _____,
PLURAL NOUN   PLURAL NOUN

to say nothing of the way they part their _____ right
NOUN

down the middle. And when they smile, believe it or not, they

have the same _____ in their teeth. They could make
NOUN

things a lot easier by _____ differently. But no,
VERB ENDING IN "ING"

they both wear the same_____ right down to their
PLURAL NOUN

matching _____. I'm telling you, no matter how
PLURAL NOUN

I try it's impossible for me to tell the difference between

_____ and _____.
PERSON IN ROOM (MALE)   PERSON IN ROOM (FEMALE)

From *Mad Libs® In Love* • Copyright © 2001 by Price Stern Sloan,
a division of Penguin Putnam Books for Young Readers, New York.

MAD LIBS® is fun to play with friends, but you can also play it by yourself! To begin with, DO NOT look at the story on the page below. Fill in the blanks on this page with the words called for. Then, using the words you've selected, fill in the blank spaces in the story.

Now you've created your own hilarious MAD LIBS® game!

HOW CAN I TELL IF SHE LIKES ME?

ADJECTIVE _____

PART OF THE BODY _____

ADVERB _____

NOUN _____

NUMBER _____

PLURAL NOUN _____

NOUN _____

NUMBER _____

NOUN _____

NOUN _____

PLURAL NOUN _____

NOUN _____

ADJECTIVE _____

NOUN _____

PART OF THE BODY _____

PLURAL NOUN _____

MAD LIBS®

HOW CAN I TELL IF SHE LIKES ME?

Keep your eyes open for these _____ signs.
ADJECTIVE

1) On your first date she fusses with her _____
PART OF THE BODY

a lot and giggles _____ at everything you say.
ADVERB

2) When you pick her up at her _____ , she keeps you
NOUN

waiting for _____ minutes. (You later learn she changed
NUMBER

her _____ ten times.)
PLURAL NOUN

3) When you're alone at a restaurant, she gets up from the

_____ every _____ minutes to visit the ladies'
NOUN   NUMBER

_____. (You can safely bet she's calling her best _____.)
NOUN   NOUN

4) She starts to flirt with other _____ when you don't
PLURAL NOUN

give her your full _____.
NOUN

5) A/An _____ friend of hers happens to run into you
ADJECTIVE

"accidentally" and tells you she thinks you're a cool _____.
NOUN

6) When she draws a/an _____ and puts her initials
PART OF THE BODY

and your _____ in it.
PLURAL NOUN

From Mad Libs® In Love • Copyright © 2001 by Price Stern Sloan,
a division of Penguin Putnam Books for Young Readers, New York.

MAD LIBS® is fun to play with friends, but you can also play it by yourself!
To begin with, DO NOT look at the story on the page below. Fill in the blanks
on this page with the words called for. Then, using the words you've selected,
fill in the blank spaces in the story.

Now you've created your own hilarious MAD LIBS® game!

HOW CAN I TELL
IF HE LIKES ME?

PLURAL NOUN _____

ADVERB _____

FRUIT _____

PART OF THE BODY _____

PLURAL NOUN _____

NOUN _____

NOUN _____

COLOR _____

NOUN _____

VERB ENDING IN "ING" _____

PART OF THE BODY _____

PLURAL NOUN _____

VERB _____

VERB _____

NOUN _____

PLURAL NOUN _____

NOUN _____

PLURAL NOUN _____

MAD☺LIBS®

HOW CAN I TELL IF HE LIKES ME?

If he exhibits three or more of the following _____ ,
PLURAL NOUN

you may _____ assume you are the _____ of his eye.
ADVERB   FRUIT

1) When you look him straight in the _____ , does he
PART OF THE BODY

avert his _____ and give you an uncomfortable _____?
PLURAL NOUN   NOUN

2) If you compliment him, does his _____ turn
NOUN

a bright _____?
COLOR

3) After you first met, did he call a mutual _____ to see
NOUN

if you were _____ steady?
VERB ENDING IN "ING"

4) When you were alone for the first time, did he try to put

his _____ around you? Did you find his _____
PART OF THE BODY   PLURAL NOUN

wet and clammy and did he sweat and _____ excessively?
VERB

5) After a passionate date, does he _____ you on the
VERB

phone or write you a/an _____ or better yet, send
NOUN

you a bouquet of _____? If he did three or more of
PLURAL NOUN

the above, you can bet your last _____ he has the
NOUN

_____ for you.
PLURAL NOUN

MAD LIBS® is fun to play with friends, but you can also play it by yourself!
To begin with, DO NOT look at the story on the page below. Fill in the blanks
on this page with the words called for. Then, using the words you've selected,
fill in the blank spaces in the story.

Now you've created your own hilarious MAD LIBS® game!

A FAN LETTER

PLURAL NOUN _____

PLURAL NOUN _____

NOUN _____

NOUN _____

ADJECTIVE _____

NOUN _____

PART OF THE BODY _____

NOUN _____

PART OF THE BODY _____

VERB _____

NOUN _____

PLURAL NOUN _____

NOUN _____

PERSON IN ROOM (FEMALE) _____

MAD LIBS®
A FAN LETTER

Dear Leonardo,

A group of my _____ and I were sitting around talking
                        PLURAL NOUN

about movie _____ and your name came up. My friend
                   PLURAL NOUN

Jenny, who really drives me up a _____, dared me to ask you
                                        NOUN

you for an autographed _____. I suppose you get zillions
                                NOUN

of _____ requests like this, but if I don't hear from you,
        ADJECTIVE

I'll be the laughing _____ of the school and Jenny will
                            NOUN

thumb her _____ at me for sure. If you do write, and
              PART OF THE BODY

hopefully you will, please, please write something personal

on your _____. I promise you, cross my _____
              NOUN   PART OF THE BODY

and hope to _____, I'll hang it in my bedroom. That way
                  VERB

your _____ will be the last thing I see before I go to sleep
        NOUN

and the first thing I see when I open my _____ in the
                                              PLURAL NOUN

morning.

Your ever faithful _____,
                        NOUN

_____
    PERSON IN ROOM (FEMALE)

MAD LIBS® is fun to play with friends, but you can also play it by yourself!
To begin with, DO NOT look at the story on the page below. Fill in the blanks
on this page with the words called for. Then, using the words you've selected,
fill in the blank spaces in the story.

Now you've created your own hilarious MAD LIBS® game!

A CASE OF PUPPY LOVE

NOUN _____

PERSON IN ROOM (MALE) _____

ANOTHER PERSON IN ROOM (MALE) _____

ADJECTIVE _____

NOUN _____

NOUN _____

NUMBER _____

VERB _____

NOUN _____

PLURAL NOUN _____

PART OF THE BODY _____

NOUN _____

VERB ENDING IN "ING" _____

ADJECTIVE _____

NOUN _____

NOUN _____

NOUN _____

NOUN _____

ADJECTIVE _____

NOUN _____

PLURAL NOUN _____

MAD☺LIBS®

A CASE OF PUPPY LOVE

(A telephone monologue to be read by a _____ in pajamas)
                                          NOUN

Hi, _____ . It's me, _____ . I hope
    PERSON IN ROOM (MALE)   ANOTHER PERSON (MALE)

I didn't wake you from a/an _____ sleep. Sure, I know
                              ADJECTIVE

what _____ it is. I have a digital _____ right by my bed.
      NOUN   NOUN

It's _____ a.m. But when I sleep over at your house, this is
     NUMBER

always the time you _____ up to go to the _____.
                     VERB   NOUN

I can't go back to sleep. I haven't even been asleep. I haven't

closed my _____ even once. Every time my
            PLURAL NOUN

_____ hits the _____ I start tossing and
PART OF THE BODY   NOUN

_____ . Nothing's the matter. I just have
VERB ENDING IN "ING"

_____ news, and I have to tell someone. My mom
ADJECTIVE

changed her _____ and said I can have a puppy, provided
              NOUN

I feed and _____-break it. I want you to go with me to the
             NOUN

shelter and pick out a -_____. I don't care what breed. It can
                        NOUN

be a cocker _____or a/an -_____ retriever or even a
              NOUN   ADJECTIVE

German _____. I'll see you first thing in the morning.
         NOUN

Go back to sleep. Try counting –_____ .
                                  PLURAL NOUN

MAD LIBS® is fun to play with friends, but you can also play it by yourself! To begin with, DO NOT look at the story on the page below. Fill in the blanks on this page with the words called for. Then, using the words you've selected, fill in the blank spaces in the story.

Now you've created your own hilarious MAD LIBS® game!

ADVICE TO THE LOVELORN

PERSON IN ROOM _____

ADJECTIVE _____

NOUN _____

PLURAL NOUN _____

ADVERB _____

ADJECTIVE _____

ADJECTIVE _____

NOUN _____

PLURAL NOUN _____

PART OF THE BODY _____

NOUN _____

PLURAL NOUN _____

SOUND _____

PLURAL NOUN _____

PLURAL NOUN _____

PERSON IN ROOM _____

Dear Dr. _____ ,
PERSON IN ROOM

I have a/an _____ problem. I finally met a/an _____
ADJECTIVE   NOUN

who is in every way the woman of my _____ .
PLURAL NOUN

She is _____ intelligent, blessed with _____ looks,
ADVERB   ADJECTIVE

and a truly _____ figure. Best of all, she has a
ADJECTIVE

remarkable sense of _____ . My problem is she also
NOUN

has two Siamese _____ , to which I am allergic.
PLURAL NOUN

Whenever I am near them, I sneeze my _____
PART OF THE BODY

off and my _____ turns red. I'd like to spend the rest
NOUN

of my life with her but not with her _____ .
PLURAL NOUN

What should I do?

Signed, Anxious

Dear Anxious,

Your situation is definitely not the cat's _____ . If your
SOUND

lady is truly attached to her _____ , you may have to
PLURAL NOUN

look for someone who has _____ for pets instead.
PLURAL NOUN

Sincerely, Dr. _____
PERSON IN ROOM

From *Mad Libs® In Love* • Copyright © 2001 by Price Stern Sloan,
a division of Penguin Putnam Books for Young Readers, New York.

MAD LIBS® is fun to play with friends, but you can also play it by yourself!
To begin with, DO NOT look at the story on the page below. Fill in the blanks
on this page with the words called for. Then, using the words you've selected,
fill in the blank spaces in the story.

Now you've created your own hilarious MAD LIBS® game!

GOOD MANNERS
MAKE GOOD SENSE

ADJECTIVE _____

ADJECTIVE _____

ADJECTIVE _____

ADJECTIVE _____

PLURAL NOUN _____

ADJECTIVE _____

ADVERB _____

ADJECTIVE _____

NOUN _____

PLURAL NOUN _____

VERB _____

NOUN _____

PART OF THE BODY _____

PLURAL NOUN _____

PLURAL NOUN _____

PART OF THE BODY _____

NOUN _____

MAD LIBS®

GOOD MANNERS MAKE GOOD SENSE

Last week, I received a/an _____ letter from a/an
ADJECTIVE

_____ reader of this _____ column. He asked
ADJECTIVEADJECTIVE

how he could make a/an _____ first impression on the
ADJECTIVE

_____ of his girlfriend. The answer is quite _____.
PLURAL NOUNADJECTIVE

All parents respond _____ to _____ manners.
ADVERBADJECTIVE

Be well mannered and they will welcome you into their

_____ with open _____. If by chance you
NOUNPLURAL NOUN

are invited to dinner, remember to never _____ with
VERB

_____ in your _____ , ever rest your
NOUNPART OF THE BODY

_____ on the table, and never, never pick
PLURAL NOUN

up _____ with your _____. Speaking of
PLURAL NOUNPART OF THE BODY

fingers, another young man recently wrote and asked   me,

"What's wrong with picking your _____ in private?"
NOUN

Everything! As I always say, good manners make good sense.

From *Mad Libs® In Love* • Copyright © 2001 by Price Stern Sloan,
a division of Penguin Putnam Books for Young Readers, New York.

MAD LIBS® is fun to play with friends, but you can also play it by yourself!
To begin with, DO NOT look at the story on the page below. Fill in the blanks
on this page with the words called for. Then, using the words you've selected,
fill in the blank spaces in the story.

Now you've created your own hilarious MAD LIBS® game!

FAIRY TALES AND ROMANCE

NOUN _____

NOUN _____

ADJECTIVE _____

PART OF THE BODY (PLURAL) _____

COLOR _____

PLURAL NOUN _____

NOUN _____

VERB ENDING IN "ING" _____

PLURAL NOUN _____

ADJECTIVE _____

ADJECTIVE _____

PLURAL NOUN _____

NOUN _____

ADJECTIVE _____

PART OF THE BODY _____

NOUN _____

NOUN _____

ADVERB _____

MAD LIBS

FAIRY TALES AND ROMANCE

If a story begins "Once upon a/an _____," you know
_____NOUN

you are about to read a fairy _____. It is amazing how
_____NOUN

these _____ stories remain indelibly etched in our
_____ADJECTIVE

_____. Who can forget Snow _____ and
PART OF THE BODY (PLURAL) _____COLOR

the Seven _____, Beauty and the _____, or
_____PLURAL NOUN _____NOUN

Little Red _____ Hood? Fairy tales introduced
_____VERB ENDING IN "ING"

us to the magical world of wicked _____ , big,
_____PLURAL NOUN

_____ wolves, _____ wizards, and dwarfs
___ADJECTIVE _____ADJECTIVE

who wore funny _____. These remarkable stories
_____PLURAL NOUN

taught us that the good always triumphs over the_____
_____NOUN

and made us believe in the _____ power of a
_____ADJECTIVE

kiss.Why not? One good smack on the _____could
_____PART OF THE BODY

change a frog into a handsome _____, enabling him to
_____NOUN

marry the _____ of his dreams and live, as is
_____NOUN

written in all these romantic stories, _____ever after.
_____ADVERB

MAD LIBS® is fun to play with friends, but you can also play it by yourself!
To begin with, DO NOT look at the story on the page below. Fill in the blanks
on this page with the words called for. Then, using the words you've selected,
fill in the blank spaces in the story.

Now you've created your own hilarious MAD LIBS® game!

SLUMBER PARTIES

WORD THAT RHYMES WITH "SUPER" _____

ADJECTIVE _____

VERB _____

PART OF THE BODY _____

ADJECTIVE _____

PLURAL NOUN _____

VERB _____

PLURAL NOUN _____

VERB ENDING IN "ING" _____

NOUN _____

PLURAL NOUN _____

ADJECTIVE _____

MAD LIBS®
SLUMBER PARTIES

In my latest book, *Super* _____
WORD THAT RHYMES WITH "SUPER"

Sleepovers, I give you over one hundred _____
ADJECTIVE

hints on how to _____ a great party.
VERB

Here are a few examples:

1) Keep it small. If it's too large, it can get out of _____ .
PART OF THE BODY

2) Plan ahead. Have a/an _____ theme and all the
ADJECTIVE

necessary _____ you'll need to _____ it off.
PLURAL NOUN   VERB

3) If you don't have enough _____ for your guests to
PLURAL NOUN

sleep in, make sure you have as many _____
VERB ENDING IN "ING"

bags as necessary.

4) Make sure there is enough food in the house to prepare a

hot _____ for your very hungry _____ .
NOUN   PLURAL NOUN

5) And most of all, remember to have a/an _____ time!
ADJECTIVE

MAD LIBS® is fun to play with friends, but you can also play it by yourself!
To begin with, DO NOT look at the story on the page below. Fill in the blanks
on this page with the words called for. Then, using the words you've selected,
fill in the blank spaces in the story.

Now you've created your own hilarious MAD LIBS® game!

WHEN YOU ARE IN LOVE . . .

NOUN _____

NOUN _____

NOUN _____

PLURAL NOUN _____

PART OF THE BODY (PLURAL) _____

NOUN _____

PLURAL NOUN _____

PART OF THE BODY _____

NOUN _____

VERB _____

PLURAL NOUN _____

NOUN _____

NOUN _____

VERB _____

NOUN _____

PLURAL NOUN _____

PART OF THE BODY _____

MAD LIBS®

WHEN YOU ARE IN LOVE...

1) You greet each day with a/an _____ in your heart
<u>NOUN</u>

and a/an _____ on your face.
<u>NOUN</u>

2) You see the whole wide _____ through rose-colored
<u>NOUN</u>

_____ and loving _____.
<u>PLURAL NOUN</u>   <u>PART OF THE BODY (PLURAL)</u>

3) You walk by a babbling _____, spontaneously remove
<u>NOUN</u>

your shoes, roll up your _____, sit down, and dangle
<u>PLURAL NOUN</u>

your _____ in the sparkling _____.
<u>PART OF THE BODY</u>   <u>NOUN</u>

4) You hug and _____ complete _____.
<u>VERB</u>   <u>PLURAL NOUN</u>

5) You believe beyond the shadow of a/an _____ that
<u>NOUN</u>

you can climb the nearest _____ or _____ the
<u>NOUN</u>   <u>VERB</u>

deepest _____.
<u>NOUN</u>

6) You feel good from the tip of your _____ to
<u>PLURAL NOUN</u>

the top of your _____.
<u>PART OF THE BODY</u>

MAD LIBS® is fun to play with friends, but you can also play it by yourself!
To begin with, DO NOT look at the story on the page below. Fill in the blanks
on this page with the words called for. Then, using the words you've selected,
fill in the blank spaces in the story.

Now you've created your own hilarious MAD LIBS® game!

ROMANTIC MOVIE BLOCKBUSTERS

ADJECTIVE _____

ADJECTIVE _____

PLURAL NOUN _____

NOUN _____

NOUN _____

NOUN _____

PLURAL NOUN _____

PLACE _____

NOUN _____

VERB _____

NOUN _____

PLURAL NOUN _____

PLURAL NOUN _____

PLURAL NOUN _____

ADJECTIVE _____

Gone With the Wind, set during the _____ War, is the
                                      ADJECTIVE

story of Scarlett O'Hara, a young, _____-willed woman.
                                      ADJECTIVE

She uses her feminine _____ to win back her _____,
                          PLURAL NOUN   NOUN

but in the process loses Rhett Butler, the only _____ she
                                                    NOUN

ever loved. Most memorable line of dialogue: "Frankly,

Scarlett, I don't give a/an _____."
                                NOUN

Rick's Café in *Casablanca* is the meeting place for _____
                                                          PLURAL NOUN

from war-torn _____. Rick sacrifices his love for Ilse
                  PLACE

when he helps her and her _____ escape the
                                NOUN

Nazis. Most memorable line: _____ it again, Sam."
                                VERB

Love Story is about two _____-league students.
                              NOUN

They go through the trials and _____
                                      PLURAL NOUN

experienced by all young _____. Unfortunately,
                              PLURAL NOUN

the ending will bring _____ to your eyes.
                          PLURAL NOUN

Most memorable line: "Love means you never have to say

you're _____."
          ADJECTIVE

From *Mad Libs® In Love* • Copyright © 2001 by Price Stern Sloan,
a division of Penguin Putnam Books for Young Readers, New York.

MAD LIBS® is fun to play with friends, but you can also play it by yourself! To begin with, DO NOT look at the story on the page below. Fill in the blanks on this page with the words called for. Then, using the words you've selected, fill in the blank spaces in the story.

Now you've created your own hilarious MAD LIBS® game!

LOVE CHAT

NOUN _____

NOUN _____

PART OF THE BODY _____

COLOR _____

NOUN _____

NOUN _____

NOUN _____

ADJECTIVE _____

NOUN _____

PERSON IN ROOM (FEMALE) _____

VERB _____

PLURAL NOUN _____

NOUN _____

My Dearest _____,
NOUN

I think of you morning, noon, and _____. I miss you
NOUN

with all my _____ . Each and every time I see
PART OF THE BODY

a/an _____-haired, _____-eyed _____
COLOR   NOUN   NOUN

I think of you. I can hardly wait for our senior _____
NOUN

Saturday night. Oops, got to go! I hear my dad coming!

He's a/an _____ sleeper and must have seen the
ADJECTIVE

_____ under my door. I'll write tomorrow.
NOUN

Love,

_____
PERSON IN ROOM (FEMALE)

P.S. Remember, if you hear about your college scholarship

you promised to _____ me immediately. I have my
VERB

_____ crossed. But I know, just know, you'll get it.
PLURAL NOUN

And even if you don't, you will always be my true _____.
NOUN

MAD LIBS® is fun to play with friends, but you can also play it by yourself!
To begin with, DO NOT look at the story on the page below. Fill in the blanks
on this page with the words called for. Then, using the words you've selected,
fill in the blank spaces in the story.

Now you've created your own hilarious MAD LIBS® game!

ASKING PERMISSION

ADVERB _____

VERB _____

VERB _____

PLURAL NOUN _____

NOUN _____

NOUN _____

ADJECTIVE _____

ADVERB _____

ADJECTIVE _____

NOUN _____

NOUN _____

PLURAL NOUN _____

NOUN _____

NOUN _____

Young man: I love your daughter _____ . I want

ADVERB

your permission to _____ her.

VERB

Father: Will you be able to _____ for my daughter

VERB

and buy her all of the _____ she needs?

PLURAL NOUN

Young man: Absolutely. Right now I'm only a junior _____

NOUN

in a prestigious _____ firm, but they tell me I have

NOUN

a/an _____ future.

ADJECTIVE

Father: Are you aware that my daughter is _____

ADVERB

opinionated and has a very _____ temper?

ADJECTIVE

Young man: Yes sir, but she's the perfect _____ for

NOUN

me. I want her to be my _____ and the mother of my

NOUN

my _____.

PLURAL NOUN

Father: Yes. I feel I'm not losing a/an _____ but

NOUN

gaining a/an _____.

NOUN

MAD LIBS® is fun to play with friends, but you can also play it by yourself!
To begin with, DO NOT look at the story on the page below. Fill in the blanks
on this page with the words called for. Then, using the words you've selected,
fill in the blank spaces in the story.

Now you've created your own hilarious MAD LIBS® game!

ROMEO AND JULIET

NOUN _____

PLURAL NOUN _____

NOUN _____

ADJECTIVE _____

PLURAL NOUN _____

ADVERB _____

PLURAL NOUN _____

PLURAL NOUN _____

PLURAL NOUN _____

FOREIGN WORD _____

VERB (PAST TENSE) _____

PLURAL NOUN _____

PLURAL NOUN _____

ADJECTIVE _____

NOUN _____

NOUN _____

LAST NAME OF PERSON IN ROOM _____

MAD❂LIBS®

ROMEO AND JULIET

If you believe William Shakespeare's *Romeo and Juliet* to be

the greatest _____ story ever written, you will not find
               NOUN

many _____ who disagree. This tragic _____
      PLURAL NOUN   NOUN

of two _____ teenagers who come from rival
        ADJECTIVE

_____ and fall _____ in love has captivated
  PLURAL NOUN   ADVERB

_____ for over four hundred _____.
  PLURAL NOUN   PLURAL NOUN

It has been translated into more than a hundred different

_____, including _____. Even those
  PLURAL NOUN   FOREIGN WORD

who have not read or _____ the play know
                        VERB (PAST TENSE)

the story of these star-crossed _____.
                                   PLURAL NOUN

Many can quote _____ from the _____
                 PLURAL NOUN   ADJECTIVE

soliloquy that Romeo delivers when he climbs a/an

_____ to get onto Juliet's _____. Scholars
  NOUN   NOUN

agree that *Romeo and Juliet* ranks up there with *Hamlet,*

Othello, and *King* _____.
                LAST NAME OF PERSON IN ROOM

From *Mad Libs® In Love* • Copyright © 2001 by Price Stern Sloan,
a division of Penguin Putnam Books for Young Readers, New York.

MAD LIBS® is fun to play with friends, but you can also play it by yourself!
To begin with, DO NOT look at the story on the page below. Fill in the blanks
on this page with the words called for. Then, using the words you've selected,
fill in the blank spaces in the story.

Now you've created your own hilarious MAD LIBS® game!

THE CRUSH

PERSON IN ROOM _____

PLURAL NOUN _____

PLURAL NOUN _____

ADJECTIVE _____

NOUN _____

NOUN _____

ADJECTIVE _____

NOUN _____

LETTER _____

NOUN _____

PART OF THE BODY _____

VERB ENDING IN "ING" _____

PLURAL NOUN _____

NOUN _____

PLURAL NOUN _____

NOUN _____

ADJECTIVE _____

NOUN _____

Hi, _____. This e-mail is for your
      PERSON IN ROOM

_____ only. You have to swear on a stack of
  PLURAL NOUN

_____ that you won't tell a single, _____
  PLURAL NOUN   ADJECTIVE

_____. You know I have this _____-size crush on
  NOUN   NOUN

the _____ hotty who sits in front of me in _____
    ADJECTIVE   NOUN

class. He's not only gorgeous, but he's a straight _____
                                        LETTER

student. He's never without a/an _____ in his
                              NOUN

_____. And he's funny. Yesterday, he had me
  PART OF THE BODY

_____ so hard that I had _____
  VERB ENDING IN "ING"   PLURAL NOUN

running down my _____. Now, here's the unbelievable part.
            NOUN

This morning I brought a pair of _____ to class and
                            PLURAL NOUN

tried to cut a lock of his _____ off. He suddenly turned
                      NOUN

and caught me _____-handed. And you know what?
                ADJECTIVE

He laughed. Then he asked me for my _____ number!
                                    NOUN

From *Mad Libs® In Love* • Copyright © 2001 by Price Stern Sloan,
a division of Penguin Putnam Books for Young Readers, New York.

MAD LIBS® is fun to play with friends, but you can also play it by yourself! To begin with, DO NOT look at the story on the page below. Fill in the blanks on this page with the words called for. Then, using the words you've selected, fill in the blank spaces in the story.

Now you've created your own hilarious MAD LIBS® game!

THE BLIND DATE

ADJECTIVE _____

NUMBER _____

ADVERB _____

NOUN _____

NOUN _____

NOUN _____

ADJECTIVE _____

NUMBER _____

ADJECTIVE _____

PLURAL NOUN _____

NOUN _____

ADVERB _____

NOUN _____

MAD LIBS®

THE BLIND DATE

Girl 1: You're home early. On a scale of one to ten, how was

your _____ date?
  ADJECTIVE

Girl 2: Minus _____!
  NUMBER

Girl 1: Laura told me he was _____ interesting.
  ADVERB

Girl 2: If you think guys who are as wide as a barn _____
  NOUN

and as short as a fire _____ are interesting. Look, I didn't
  NOUN

expect him to be a Greek _____, but I certainly didn't
  NOUN

count on him being an animal.

Girl 1: What did you do?

Girl 2: We ate. No, he ate. He had a/an _____
  ADJECTIVE

pizza with _____ toppings, three _____ hamburgers,
  NUMBER   ADJECTIVE

and a double order of French _____. Then we went to
  PLURAL NOUN

a movie where he ate a family-sized _____ of popcorn, and
  NOUN

he burped _____ through the whole thing.
  ADVERB

Girl 1: Are you going to see him again?

Girl 2: Of course. Wednesday we're going to a Chinese

_____ for dinner.
  NOUN

MAD LIBS® is fun to play with friends, but you can also play it by yourself!
To begin with, DO NOT look at the story on the page below. Fill in the blanks
on this page with the words called for. Then, using the words you've selected,
fill in the blank spaces in the story.

Now you've created your own hilarious MAD LIBS® game!

FIVE TIPS FOR A
PERFECT WEDDING

ADJECTIVE _____

NOUN _____

NOUN _____

NOUN _____

NOUN _____

NOUN _____

ADJECTIVE _____

PLURAL NOUN _____

PLURAL NOUN _____

COLOR _____

PLURAL NOUN _____

COLOR _____

PLURAL NOUN _____

NUMBER _____

NUMBER _____

PLURAL NOUN _____

PLURAL NOUN _____

VERB _____

NOUN _____

NOUN _____

ADJECTIVE _____

FIVE TIPS FOR A
PERFECT WEDDING

1. The bride should always wear a/an _____
                                        ADJECTIVE

_____, the groom a/an _____ .
        NOUN   NOUN

2. The bride's _____ should always pay for the
                     NOUN

_____, while the _____ of the groom should
      NOUN   NOUN

pick up the tab for the _____ dinner the night
                              ADJECTIVE

before the wedding.

3. One color scheme should be followed when choosing the

_____ as well as the _____. For example,
   PLURAL NOUN   PLURAL NOUN

if you choose _____ _____ , then you should
                  COLOR   PLURAL NOUN

have _____ _____ .
        COLOR   PLURAL NOUN

4. The bride should choose _____ to _____ of her closest
                              NUMBER   NUMBER

_____ to be her attendants. The groom should choose
  PLURAL NOUN

the same number of his _____ to be the groomsmen.
                              PLURAL NOUN

5. Guests should remember to _____ on time.
                                   VERB

Remember it's the _____ and _____'s _____
                      NOUN   NOUN   ADJECTIVE

day, and you don't want to ruin it!